THE ASTHMATIC GLASSBLOWER

the ASTHMATIC

BILLEH
NICKERSON

GLASSBLOWER
and other poems

Arsenal Pulp Press
Vancouver

THE ASTHMATIC GLASSBLOWER
AND OTHER POEMS
Copyright © 2000 by Billeh Nickerson

ARSENAL PULP PRESS
103-1014 Homer Street
Vancouver, B.C.
Canada V6B 2W9
www.arsenalpulp.com

The publisher gratefully acknowledges the support of the Canada Council for the Arts and the B.C. Arts Council for its publishing program, and the support of the Government of Canada through the Book Publishing Industry Development Program for its publishing activities.

Designed by Solo
Printed and bound in Canada

CANADIAN CATALOGUING IN PUBLICATION DATA:
Nickerson, Billeh, 1972 –
  The asthmatic glassblower and other poems

  ISBN 1-55152-088-5

I. Title.
PS8577.I32A92 2000   C811'.6   C00-911003-8
PR9199.3.N4975A92 2000

For all the girls I've loved before

SOMETIMES GAY MEANS HAPPY

THE ASTHMATIC GLASSBLOWER
and other poems

SOMETIMES GAY MEANS HAPPY

*Sometimes I'm certain those who are happy
know one thing more than us . . . or one thing less.*

— Anne Michaels

The push of knowing
you're different,
the pull of wanting
to belong.

OSTRICH

Crossed my legs, wore baggy pants,
pulled my sweater down, covered myself
with blankets, pillows, jackets,
sat with the cat on my lap,
my lunch bag, my knapsack,
as if my cock were hidden
beneath the earth,
the rest of me convinced
no one could see.

LOUISVILLE SLUGGER

Think baseball he tells me
but it's difficult
on hands and knees –
the same way I'd play
horseback riding
when my sister was five
& I was nine.
Think baseball and I knew
it would come to this,
a day when I let this happen,
but I never thought I'd be
thinking baseball,
my uncles during the World Series,
my stiff leather mitt,
my grade eight gym class when
even the teacher laughed
because I threw
like a girl.

BEING A FAGGOT

Being a faggot means you can wear
the tightest underwear, bathe
in the hottest hot tubs
without having to worry
about sperm counts.

Being a faggot means you can laugh
at divorce rates, the couple
on top of wedding cakes;
being a faggot means
you're a perpetual best man.

Being a faggot means you get to
hear about everyone else's
faggot friends and sometimes
their faggot uncles.

Being a faggot means you can drink
homo milk without being embarrassed.

Being a faggot means you get invited to
baby showers, lesbian potlucks – or
lesbian potluck baby showers where
you're the donating father.

Being a faggot means you pay
into the policy
without extending the benefits.

Being a faggot means
your blood isn't good enough.

Being a faggot means
you'll still fall in love
with straight men.

IN THE SHOWER

My lover feeds me mango
with his switchblade
close against my lips.
This is when my tongue
glides easiest,
licks strings of fruit
off our skin,
into my mouth.

I want to tell him –
warm water trickling
down our backs,
my thumbs circling
his nipples –
I'm afraid the blade
might slip

but there's so much
being said right now
as he thrusts the fruit
against my stomach,
guts it
like a small animal.

WHY I LOVE WAYNE GRETZKY –
AN EROTIC FANTASY

Because he knows what to do with pucks,
slapshots, wristshots, all that intricate stickwork
as he slips through defencemen,
shoots between the legs
& scores.

Because he likes to pretend
I'm the zamboni & he
the filthy ice.

Because even if he's tired
he'll perk up
whenever I sing *O Canada*.

Because sometimes my dyslexia makes me see
a giant 69 on his back.

Because he's always ready for overtime –
because he never shoots then snores.

Because he understands the importance of
a good organ player.

Because he calls me his stick boy.

Because he likes to be tied-up
with the laces from his skates.

Because behind every great man
it feels good.

DRIVING IN ADAM'S JEEP

I keep praying red lights,
the hum of his transmission
when his hand gears down,
almost touches my knee.
Seatbelts aren't the only form
of restraint.
On nights like this –
the wet asphalt making me
lick my lips –
I want him to kiss me
with the windshield wipers on.

\\Kiss me//

\\Kiss me//

\\Kiss me//

✝

if you bite your tongue
long enough
it will bleed   everything
you kept yourself
from saying

ALREADY TEN LOVERS

I have run out of fingers.
There was a time I'd name them,
this one Cameron, this one Sam,
but does it matter anymore?
It's like my grade one math class
when my fingers become too few
for the equations.

I wonder if it's worthwhile
keeping track,
my toes more important
than they should be,
eleven never this significant.

Poem For My Foreskin

It's not as if we were given a chance,
everyone else decided
we needed to be separated –
like children always up to conspiracies,
too much fun together.

I didn't know you were missing
until I asked my mother
why Nazis made men drop their pants,
my body all of a sudden lacking,
no longer whole.

Sometimes I try to remind myself,
pull skin down around my penis,
but I can never remember you
even though some psychologists believe
I'm still traumatized by the pain
the day the doctor sliced you.

The first time I slept with
an uncircumcised man
I wanted to ask him
what you'd have been like,
my fingers feeling on him
the closest
I'll ever get to you.

GONORRHEA

If I could pinpoint my shame
to one precise moment
it wouldn't be the sex or
the first stains on my underwear.
It wouldn't be the day I walked to
the Public Library too embarrassed
to ask for assistance
or pulling out my cock
while the doctor told army stories,
his family looking down at me
from a framed photograph,
ten of them on a stairwell,
eight children, the mother
and the doctor.
If I could pinpoint my shame,
thumb tack it
to the cork message board
of my youth,
it would be the moment
I made him a girl,
told the doctor I couldn't remember
her name or where she lived
though she mentioned something
about the East, missing
her parents and the snow.

IF YOU FIT ALL YOUR LOVERS IN AN AIRPLANE, WHAT KIND OF AIRPLANE WOULD IT BE?

In my dreams it's a 747 filled
with sports teams,
baseball, football, soccer –
anything with balls, basically.
I'm the Captain, of course,
which means I just stick it
on automatic, head back
into the cabin to take
frequent flyer applications
in the rear.

One day it could be a 737
with enough seats
for each of my lovers
to hold one of Disney's
101 Dalmatians.
At first, I'd name each pup
after the lap it sits on
but then there'd be so many Jasons
and Chrises
and Brads
that I'd just refer to them by number.

Right now I'd need a turboprop commuter,
one of those short haul affairs
with thirty seats and a flight attendant
who gives you a phone number
if you're lucky,
honey roasted peanuts
if you're not.

How strange it seems
I once started off
in a twinseater,
no carry-on baggage,
just me and the pilot exploring
the various landscapes until
our single-engine sputters
and I realize I can never fly
in such a small plane again.

when he rolled the penny
around my penis
maple leaf   queen
tails   then   heads
I didn't give a damn
where that penny had been

It's Hard to Say No

When he kisses with his eyes closed,
when he calls you his Greek god,
when he lets you cheat at Scrabble,
when he reminds you of an ex,
when he smells like vanilla,
when he pets your cat,
when he breathes,
when he blinks,
when he hums while shaving,
when he makes banana pancakes,
when he fingers his nipples,
when he trims your hair – just a little,
when he talks like Donald Duck,
when he sucks on your chin,
when he tickles,
when he nibbles.
when he washes the windows,
when he knows the names of all seven dwarfs,
when he burns the waffles,
when he pulls your leg,
when he eats your sins,
when he swallows
                          your pain.

Nadine's Brass Bed

For years Nadine's brass bed
moved around our building
like a cat
always finding itself a new home
as tenants backpacked Europe,
taught English in the East,
or, simply, started anew.

It was always someone else's turn
to make it their own, break it down
in one apartment so
it could be rebuilt in another,
the shine of its finish
reflecting around the room as
we washed our hands
of a greenish hue
one more time.

I've often wondered how many of us
have experienced its squeak,
the way it amplifies your passion
without apology,
announces it to the world
whether you want it to or not.

How different to make love
on something so full of history
instead of the futons our parents bought
or the old foam mattresses
left over from our youth.

To make love on Nadine's brass bed
was to make love to ritual,
your fists grasped so tight
around its bars,
when you finally let go
you could see yourself
from above.

His First Time

When it's his first time with a guy
& you've wanted this to happen
for so long
even when everyone else said
he's straighter than an arrow
but you knew & now all he wants is
to make you come
but it's hard
'cuz you've had so much to drink
& he doesn't really know
what he's doing –
just sucks and sucks
with such urgency
you're not sure
what he'll pull
from your body.

Later you'll tell your friend you got
sucked off for half an hour
but you'll neglect to tell her
you wanted to stop
that it wasn't fair to either of you
that it shouldn't have happened that way
but you're happy   for him
& maybe
he'll call
tomorrow.

There's a trick
with a dick
I'm learning to do.

Park Poems

told him my name was todd   that I was new at this
and nervous   we used my trench coat as a blanket
I never looked at him   just the sky   it reminded me
of camping   I hadn't stared at the stars like that in a
long time

< >

all around the world
men in jogging suits
pretending to be
joggers

< >

it's as if they're a totem pole
one man on his knees
the other standing tall
his face distorted

You Can Stick Your Dick in Me

You can stick your dick in me.
Sure, I'll go all the way
just to make you happy.

My first time on hands and knees
and what should I say?
You can stick your dick in me

if you're gentle, please,
'cause I'm more than a lay
just to make you happy.

I thought this would be the key
to what it means to be gay –
you can stick your dick in me,

set my true self free –
but right now, today,
it's just to make you happy.

Let's pretend I'm full of glee
and love is here to stay.
You can stick your dick in me
just to make you happy.

GUY WITH THE REALLY BIG NOSE

I feel like I should know his name,
should be able to see it spelled out
on that small white rectangle but
I remember only his really big nose
pressed against my cheek when we kissed,
how I placed his business card in a book
as if I were pressing a flower,
and that since I forgot that book's title
I think of him each time
I turn a page
and something falls out.

Apparently

You lose part of yourself each time
you sleep with someone
or that's what my friend believes

which is fine for her since
she hasn't slept with a lot of people
but since I have I needed to ask her

what exactly it is I lose
and how exactly I lose it.
She said you just lose

a piece of yourself, a something
you're never really sure what,
but, like after a broke bone,

you're never the same again
no matter how hard you try
otherwise.

Not Another AIDS Poem

You can write about being gay,
your first *partner*, the wonders of
coming out to friends and family,
but you're not supposed to write about
fistfucking,
his wristwatch taking a licking
as it keeps on ticking
inside of you
like
a heartbeat.

Please tell me I'm not
the kind of person
who fucks
without a condom
then drives home
wearing a seatbelt.

At the Martial Arts Cinema

When the villain pulls
his victim's heart out –

when the villain pulls
his victim's heart out
barehanded –

when the villain pulls
his victim's heart out
barehanded,
the muscle throbbing –

when the villain pulls
his victim's heart out
barehanded,
the muscle throbbing
while its owner watches
I can't stop thinking about it

because I know
it could happen
to me

again.

THE ULTRA CENTRIFUGE

When I asked my lover what he'd done that day
    I wanted him to ask me too
since I'd just bought groceries and felt really proud,
    but instead of the usual summations,
the subsequent kiss, he just stood there, told me
    he spun people's blood all day,

tube after tube in the ultra centrifuge.
    I'd never heard of a centrifuge before
but I liked its sound so while my lover explained
    how it spins fast enough to make HIV
separate from plasma like cream gathering atop
    an old fashioned milk bottle

I practiced pronouncing it the same way
    I repeat the names to foreign places
in case I ever go there: ul-tra cen-tri-fuge,
    ultra centrifuge, ultra centrifuge spinning
inside my mouth, my tongue separating
    each word by syllabic weight.

My lover said it's easy when you don't know
    their faces, when you don't see them
exit the clinic doors with Band-Aids
    on short-sleeved arms, when you can't feel
the warmth of their just given blood
    through your latex gloves and glass tubes.

That evening while my lover lay beside me
    I wondered how it felt
to hold the blood between his fingers,
    whether he learned to hold
my cock from holding test tubes
    or test tubes from my cock.

Dildos Don't Float

We'd just broken up and I'd come home
to find two dinks in the sink.
I didn't know what to think at first,
whether he intended to hurt me or
whether he thought it a good time
to start spring cleaning.
All I knew was two miniature pink torpedoes
sat useless in the bathroom sink
where I wash my hands.
I wanted to tell him
to go fuck himself
but it was obvious he already had
so I just stood there for a minute
then walked past the La-Z-Boy where he sat
to the sink in the kitchen.
I guess I can't complain too much,
at least he's hygienic, but how telling
that when our ship finally sank
it wasn't the rats that jumped first,
rather two plastic peckers.
It's the last thing he taught me,
dildos don't float, numb and heavy,
they just sit there,
the desire spent.

†

If only relationships
came complete
with intermittent red lights,
like on smoke detectors,
so we could see
when the love runs out.

LAST CALL MEANS I LOVE YOU

This morning I felt as if I'd become old like
those men last night offering to buy drinks,
their conversation riddled with silence,
long swigs of cheap bottled beer.
There was a time I'd take comfort
the only thing I'd brought home was
the smell of smoke and sweat, but now
I've begun to understand why men stand
hours with their backs to the wall,
how strangers can make you feel
beautiful again, wanted,
less lonely.

FEBRUARY

I

what the green apple thought
when the unripe bananas
competed for yellow

2

At the Greasy Spoon

The waitress tells me
her pitbull was impregnated
by a husky.
This makes my grilled-cheese
taste better.
It really does.

3

Upon Leaving Home

I wonder if my mother
still dreams inventions
for spill-proof
children's bubbles.

4

the way bus drivers
wave to anything
larger than a pick-up

5

Personal Secret #43

When I'm depressed
I say "Lola Falana"
over and over
until everything
seems normal again.

6

Most of my straight friends
have gay uncles.

7

Swimming Lessons

Her feet on concrete,
the raised triangle
between her legs.

8

1500 Q-Tips

My mother keeps sending
care packages –
if I used one Q-Tip everyday
I'd have enough for four years.

9

wind chimes during hurricanes

10

What About Cabbage?

Tonight, I dreamt
I was arrested
for planting carrots
in cemeteries.

11

wet asphalt makes me
lick my lips

12

My Boyfriend's Back

I pluck a hair
with my teeth,
swallow the evidence.

13

Gilligan's Island

I want to stick my fingers
inside Mary Ann's
coconut cream pie.

14

On the Bus

A woman keeps shooting me
with her blue dolphin.
She squints one eye, then pulls
the dorsal fin.

15

I'm bobbing for apples,
bobbing for apples.
His hands push my head
down lower.

16

During Chad's Funeral

There is nothing partial
about semi-trailers,
nothing kind-of, somewhat
or half-assed at all.

17

silence is a goldfish

18

Nude Bingo

The old dab-your-wiener trick,
how original.

19

the sound of your sigh
when the buttered bread
lands right-side up

20

Tips for Pedestrians

You've got to turn your back
on the big trucks –
gravel shoots like bullets.

21

black women in wheelchairs
rolling through the dreams
of corporate executives

22

it always comes down to up   the ass

23

Racist Eating French Vanilla

Something is wrong,
it's not white.

24

Looking Back

Kissed him with my eyes closed,
my mouth far too open.
I liked to ask him if he was hard
even when my fingers knew.

25

I'm searching for someone
to wear black with me.

26

like papercuts
pampas grass
surprises me

27

Jesus couldn't get a job
at McDonald's –
his hair is too long.

28

Every spider you've killed,
every web you've vacuumed.

29

so full of drunk love
I hug myself
harder and harder
until I disappear

PERSUADING THE IMAGINARY

FOCUS

Since describing emotion is very difficult
leaf through some newspapers
to find a picture.
A photograph of a boy looking
at his broken bicycle
might suggest bewilderment,
anger or frustration.
Try to choose a picture which
portrays clearly one emotion.
It's not necessary that you tell
a story; the creation of mood is
the important thing.
Consider love, hate, anger, joy,
disappointment, hope, rage and ecstasy.

Found poem from "Let's Get Involved," a section of
Walter R. Bremner's Focus, *one of my high school English textbooks.*

PRIMARY

Trina cut and pasted bras
from clothing catalogues,
called them butterflies
fluttering around
a necktie road, a T-shirt forest,
and a peach-coloured sun –
yellow wasn't fashionable.

I remember the teacher,
how Trina cried
they're butterflies
they're butterflies
and how Barry stuck his finger
into the glue, licked it
when no one was looking.

KINDERGARTEN

Kelly Berry had red hair.

Chrissy McCombie had blue eyes.

Shannon Breeze figure skated.

Tammy didn't talk a lot.

Barry Thornaloe sang *Twinkle Twinkle Little Star* in the bathroom.

Lesley Leedum kicked hard.

Pam Reimer had three older sisters.

Michelle Aspinal's father was a doctor.

One of the Jasons never showed again.

Jeremiah stepped on ants.

Steven Kitson limped.

I couldn't tie my shoelaces yet.

Mrs. Marten could.

Grade Two

My mother and her family used to skate around
bonfires on frozen lakes. She used to describe their
sing-a-longs, the taste of their hot chocolate and all the
silly things her brothers did but I never paid attention
to that. Just knowing my mother could have fallen
through, her family forced to make a human chain,
Uncle John's outreached hand just able to pull her out,
really excited me. During my one trip to Nova Scotia
when the lakes were frozen enough to skate on, Aunt
Martha told me to be careful because a young boy had
fallen through the ice that week and they still hadn't
found his body. For weeks after my skate I had night-
mares of the young boy's mother roaming the halls of
my school checking every corner for a lost and found
box, the one containing her son.

CATERPILLAR SLIVERS

My sister never understood why
my father cut tree branches
filled with caterpillar nests.
She liked to make friends with them,
name them after adjectives: *fuzzy, fluffy*
sometimes she'd call them *velvet*.
I once tried to explain how
their furry bodies had fooled her,
how they were nature's first
lumberjacks, their chainsaw jaws
eating their way through forests,
but she wouldn't believe me.
She was content with them
crawling up and down her arms,
their sharp-tipped hairs
tickling her,
imbedding themselves
deep into her skin.

Grade Four

Miss Mills said the bake sale would be on a Thursday so if we didn't sell everything right away we could sell it the day after. If everyone brought six cupcakes we'd have enough to hire a real Indian to talk about real Indian stuff like pemmican and teepees and bison – not buffalo. Most of the cupcakes sold for twenty-five cents but since Kathy's dad was a baker and hers had lots of icing they sold for more. The Indian danced in real Indian head gear and sang real Indian songs about his people. A couple kids laughed because you could see his bum in the loincloth. Some kids brought their moms.

GRADE FIVE

In grade five they taught us
certain drugs could make you think
you were Superman.
This always fascinated me, innocent
teenagers thinking they could fly,
dancing around rooftops, open windows,
the high beams to bridges.

During Saturday morning cartoons
it was difficult not to think
of the teachers' warnings.
While Superman leapt over buildings
in a single bound,
I thought of all the wannabe Supermans
and the pavement
so unforgiving
beneath them.

Farrah Fawcett

Farrah Fawcett's teeth were big and white   bigger
than Donny Osmond's   even bigger than Marie's
Farrah Fawcett's teeth were so big they became a
question on Family Feud   Richard Dawson asking
contestants to name a celebrity with big teeth and me
thinking Farrah Fawcett   once at my dentist's office
the dental hygienist said I should floss more or my
teeth would fall out   all I could think about was
Farrah Fawcett   her pearly whites   her imminent
divorce from the Six-Million-Dollar Man   and my
friend Jason saying he'd seen her pussy on Charlie's
Angels   but I didn't believe him because Charlie's
Angels was in English and they only showed pussies
on the French channel

JINKIES
(for Velma)

It must have been difficult to be a stereotype,
the token smart chick with glasses, the one
always depended on, the one taken for granted.
In the backseat of the Mystery Machine
you dreamt of being up front with Fred,
his body covered in the orange lint
of your turtleneck sweater;
no Daphne, no Shaggy, no Scooby-Doo,
or those ridiculous Scooby snacks,
just the two of you and the Mystery Machine
filled with sleeping bags.
Sure, they loved you
when there was a mystery to solve
but you wondered about the day
the mysteries stopped,
the only mystery that mattered.

GRADE NINE

We learned the Russians had a nuclear missile aimed at the airport across the street from our high school because it was far enough out of range from the big city that airplanes could still land after a nuclear attack. My friend Jason said we were lucky, we'd just be vapourized while others would have to live through a nuclear winter. I wasn't sure what that meant but I pictured it cold and dark, like Siberia, only in my own town. Whenever a teacher announced USSR – United Sustained Silent Reading – I'd hum along with the airplanes and think of Russia, how easily we could all disappear.

Three's Company

Larry wouldn't talk about it,
the time he and Janet and Jack
drank too much, found themselves
in the same bed together –
his hands on Janet's hips,
his lips pressed against Jack's.

Janet knew Chrissy wouldn't understand
how good it felt
when she lay between them –
the way their chest hairs
and gold chains
tickled her nipples.
She wondered what Cosmo would say,
whether this was a good or
a bad girl thing.

Jack thought of it often,
like a favourite spice you want
added to everything.
He experimented with recipes,
new flavours, new textures.
He couldn't stop craving.
He always licked the spoon.

From Mrs. Roper's Diary: For Stanley

When the tenants upstairs make love
I close my eyes and pretend
their sounds come from us –
the days I'd dress up
like Little Red Riding Hood,
my picnic basket filled
with cherries
as he'd sneak up behind me,
huff and puff and blow
the house down.

Sometimes he'd be Little Jack Horner
always pulling plums out
with his thumb
or Papa Bear mixing his far too hot
with my Mama Bear cold.
Who needs Goldilocks
to make everything feel just right?

Now, I'm wondering
if this is our storybook ending?
When did happily ever after
mean sleeping with throw pillows
in between us?
When did other people's passion
substitute our own?

Janet's Flower Shop

Like a high school football star
who buys a car lot,
his every sale a private touchdown,
Janet's plants became pirouettes,
her feet as light as rose petals
as she danced
from customer to customer.

Grade Ten

A bunch of grade twelves told everyone they sneaked
into a bar downtown and saw a stripper shoot a popsi-
cle from between her legs out into the audience. At first
I didn't believe them, but then I saw the towel they
brought back. An ordinary towel. The kind you buy at
white sales. They kept sniffing it and stroking it as if it
were she. Only the cool guys or younger brothers of
cool guys were allowed to hold it. I was lucky just to
see it. For some reason I've always pictured the popsicle
as being orange, though they never told us what flavour
she used.

Homage

1
During the summer when sleep-overs were dangerous,
my mother hid my favourite shirt.
The news said names were important,
the velvet letters on my chest,
the B- I- L- L- Y,
A way for the bad man
to get to know me.

I though the children who went missing
had stupid mothers –
they never took the shirt-with-the-name away.

2
I still see their pictures on milk cartons,
convenience store windows,
airport departure lounges
(never arrivals).

From time to time
their images are age-enhanced,
computers predicting
a few teeth, a new smile –
one with or without the gaps.

3
When your child goes missing,
becomes *still born* at the age of seven,
even steam rising from a coffee cup
reminds you of mornings
you'd sit together:

his uneaten toast crusts,
the smell of his hot chocolate,
his envious eyes as you sipped
your grown-up's coffee.

LADYBUG

I am a blood drop angel, a speck
from Dorothy's ruby slippers. I fly
through the air like a chip of cherry
nail polish with wings. I am the eye
of a raspberry flecked with ink,
the first taste from Persephone's
pomegranate, a piece of broken heart
littered with poppy seeds.

The Chinchilla Farmer's Son

Your father skinned rabbits
while your mother sprinkled cinnamon
over pie shells filled with apples.
He wore aprons when he barbecued,
smeared Heinz 57 sauce
with short-bristle brushes
reminding you of magic wands.
He was a magician,
the rabbits collapsible top hats
his strong hands could reach into.
This was impressive,
but you had your own trick.
Your eyes could make
caged chinchillas move.

So while your mother sprinkled cinnamon,
your father pulling out rabbits,
you were blinking the chinchillas,
the chickens, the mailbox,
back and forth,
across the farm

THE ASTHMATIC GLASSBLOWER

When I was five, I decided
to become a glassblower.
My mother was thrilled.
She believed *no* was a terrible word,
that imagination could cure
better than medicine.

It didn't matter I couldn't
even blow bubbles, always
inhaling the soapy film of
my bubble wand, then
coughing and wheezing until
I had to use my ventolin.

What mattered was when my fingers
pretended to roll a small metal tube
 − my lips puckered just so −
my mother could see what I was shaping:
my fragile breath was willing
the glass, persuading the imaginary
into a perfect, pink lung.

Acknowledgments

Some of the poems in this book have appeared or are forthcoming in the following magazines: *Canadian Forum, Capilano Review, The Church-Wellesley Review, Contemporary Verse 2, Front, Geist, Monday Magazine, The New Quarterly*, and *Prism international*; and in the anthologies *Chasing Halley's Comet* and *Hammer and Tongs: a Smoking Lung Anthology*. Thank you for supporting my work.

Some of these poems received an Award of Special Recognition at the 1995 BC Festival of the Arts.

Many poems in the "Sometimes Gay Means Happy" section were published in a chapbook of the same name by Smoking Lung Press in 1997.

This book would not have been possible without support from the following individuals: Brian Lam and Blaine Kyllo at Arsenal Pulp, my editor Patrick Lane, the incomparable Lorna Crozier, Aislinn Hunter, Brad Cran, Chris Hutchinson, Craig Moseley, Heather Macleod, Shane Book, Sheri-D Wilson, Stephen Osborne, and Teresa McWhirter. You all rock my world.

Thank you also to Ana Tores, Barbara Zatyko,
bill bissett, Colette Parras, Frédéric Zalac,
Gregory Scofield, Iyko Day, Jane Southwell Munro,
Jason Thompson, Joan Stewart, Lynn Crosbie,
Michael V. Smith, Mark Cochrane, Miranda Pearson,
Pamela Donoghue, Pascal Milelli, Patty Osborne,
Rebecca Fredrickson, Richard Van Camp, Rose Firth,
Roseanne Harvey, Ryan Knighton, Sam Boonstra,
Stephen Hume, my fellow students at the University
of Victoria Writing department, The BC Arts Council
Scholarship Program, and Smoking Lung Press.

Billeh Nickerson was born on Valentine's Day, 1972, in Halifax, Nova Scotia. He grew up in Langley, BC, and now lives in Vancouver where he is a contributing editor to *Geist* magazine. His column, "Hard Core Homo" appears monthly in *Xtra! West*.